Side Hustle Secrets
Wealth-Building Strategies for the Ambitious

Table of Contents

Chapter 1. Introduction

In this exciting Special Report, we delve into the fascinating world of side hustles with our exclusive piece, "Side Hustle Secrets: Wealth-Building Strategies for the Ambitious." Feel a surge of inspiration as we unpack the secrets of successful wealth-builders who turned their passions into profit. Unearth the potential you never knew you had as we guide you through comprehensive wealth-building strategies, tailored for the ambitious and driven individuals. Whether you're looking to create a secondary income stream or dreaming about becoming your own boss, this report could well be the gateway to your financial independence. Ready to turn your entrepreneurial dreams into reality? This Special Report is your ticket to a better financial future. Don't miss out! Your wealth-building journey begins here. Invest in this report, invest in yourself.

Chapter 2. Unveiling the Side Hustle Phenomenon

Every ambitious wealth-builder holds an unturned stone within their reach that often goes unrecognized. This stone is commonly referred to as the "side hustle". It has been the vehicle to financial independence for countless entrepreneurs. Serving as a supplement to a full-time job or as the springboard into full-scale entrepreneurship; the side hustle phenomenon has, and continues to shape the financial landscapes of millions globally.

2.1. Rooted in History, Blossoming in the Present

The concept of side hustling is not contemporary. In fact, its roots are firmly grounded in history. The blacksmiths of old would often mend shoes or make household goods in addition to forging weapons. Farmers would repair tools and sell hand-carved objects. Fast-forward to the present, this phenomenon has merely adopted a new lexicon and broadened its reach. Thanks to the internet and the digital revolution, side hustling has evolved from local to global, knocking geographic barriers out of its path. From podcasting to freelance writing, from digital marketing consultation to e-commerce businesses, the opportunities are vast and diverse.

2.2. The Essentials of Side Hustling

Embarking on a side hustle journey involves a significant degree of understanding and preparation. Attempting to juggle it with full-time commitments without a well-charted plan could end in chaos. Here, we spell out the essentials of a side hustle:

1. ***Identification:*** The first and most crucial step is identifying your talents, skills, and passions. Selection should be centered around something you are both good at, and enjoy doing. This often ensures a greater degree of resilience when challenges arise.

2. ***Market Demand:*** Gauge the market for your offering. Understanding your potential customers, their needs and their behavior will contribute towards shaping your side hustle's direction.

3. ***Plan:*** A well-structured blueprint will help navigate the side hustle landscape. Goals, timelines, workload management, and financial projections - these are some parameters to consider when planning your side hustle.

4. ***Execution:*** To gain momentum, it's vital to act with determination and consistency. Experiment, learn from failure, and optimize for success.

2.3. The Power of Diversified Income

A significant advantage of side hustles is the diversification of income. It provides a safety net, minimizing the risks associated with reliance on one income source. Consider it as a personal insurance policy against financial hiccups. Plus, diversification also presents opportunities for accelerated wealth building. The extra income can be reinvested, creating additional streams of revenue.

2.4. The Freedom Factor

The side hustle symbolizes freedom, not just in financial terms but also at a personal level. It allows you to explore interests outside your regular employment, cultivating creativity, and providing a sense of fulfillment. This freedom often translates to increased confidence and improved well-being.

2.5. Community and Networking

Side hustles can provide access to diverse communities and networking opportunities. Interaction with like-minded individuals, potential clients, or mentors can lead to meaningful relationships. These relationships often prove instrumental in fueling the success of your side hustle.

2.6. Leaving Room for Growth

The end goal for any side hustle is to see growth, whether it's in terms of revenue, customer base, or reputation. Therefore, whenever planning your side hustle, it's crucial to ensure it holds potential for scalability. Freshness in offerings, leveraging technology, and understanding market trends can aid scalability.

2.7. Case In Point: Success Stories

There is no dearth of entrepreneurs who kicked off their financial journey with side hustles. From Steve Jobs kickstarting Apple in his parents' garage to the creators of Airbnb testing the idea by renting out their living room space; the side hustle world holds countless inspiring success stories that speak to its potential.

In conclusion, the side hustle reverberates the song of independence and empowerment. It provides the opportunity to turn interests into income, dreams into reality. The phenomenon of side hustling emerged not merely as a trend, but as an essential component of wealth-building; one with the potential to shape the future of work and entrepreneurship. So get ready, stay determined and welcome to the exciting world of side hustling!

Chapter 3. Testing Your Side Hustle Idea: A Roadmap

Understanding the potential of your side hustle idea is crucial before diving headfirst into the venture. This extensive roadmap will guide you on how to analyze and evaluate your side hustle idea to ensure its feasibility and profitability.

3.1. Identifying Your Side Hustle

The first step is to identify what your side hustle would be. Your side hustle should reflect your skills, passion, or a niche you've identified in the market. Methods to help with this brainstorming process include:

1. Listing your skills, interests, and experience

2. Identifying where those skills might be utilizable and marketable

3. Researching trends and opportunities in the market

4. Evaluating whether any niche areas are underserved in the market

Take the time to let ideas simmer and select only a few to move forward with for the next stages.

3.2. Market Research

Once you have a grasp on what your side hustle could be, the next step is to conduct market research. This involves looking at the competition, assessing demand, and understanding potential customers. Some steps to effectively carry out this analysis include:

1. Look into direct and indirect competitors in a similar field

2. Identify the strengths and weaknesses of these competitors

3. Evaluate demand for your product or service

4. Understand the preferences and behavior of your potential customers

3.3. Validation Process

Now it's time to validate your idea to understand whether your target market would be interested in your side hustle. Tools for this include:

1. Surveys and questionnaires

2. Pilot tests or trials

3. Feedback from focus groups or beta testers

The data garnered can help you confirm whether your idea is something to invest time and resources into. You get a sense of interest levels, potential pricing strategies, and audience responses.

3.4. Assessing the Financial Feasibility

A side hustle is meant to be a profitable venture. Therefore, assessing the financial feasibility of your idea is critical. You can do this by:

1. Estimating your startup costs

2. Predicting your potential income from the side hustle

3. Assessing the time and financial commitment necessary

4. Understanding the tax implications of your side hustle

If the numbers don't add up or profits seem unrealistic, it might be time to reassess or adjust your side hustle idea.

3.5. Building a Business Model

Your business model is a roadmap of how you intend to operate profitably. Components to craft include:

1. What your product/service is

2. Who your customers are

3. How you'll reach your customers

4. How you'll retain and nurture your customer base

5. Sources of revenue and expenses

This step is a significant determinant of the survival of your side hustle.

3.6. Building Your Minimal Viable Product

The term minimal viable product (MVP) refers to the most basic version of your product that solves the problem for users effectively.

1. Identify the core functionality of your product

2. Test this core product in a small but targeted group

3. Receive feedback and iterate on it continually

The faster you're able to iterate and improve your MVP, the better chances you have at success.

3.7. Constructing a Marketing Strategy

A robust marketing strategy ensures that your side hustle reaches your target audience. Key components necessary to craft your marketing strategy include:

1. Understanding and defining your marketing channels (social media, email marketing, SEO, etc.)

2. Cultivating a solid online presence

3. Creating an engaging brand

Always iterate, optimize, and test new tactics.

Adhering to the steps of this roadmap will ensure that your side hustle idea is tested and vetted properly. Make informed decisions based on thorough research and objective evaluation, and you're on your way to building a successful side hustle.

Chapter 4. Laying a Solid Foundation: Setting Your Goals

Before we delve into the lucrative business ideas and hacks you can employ to start your lucrative side hustle, it's crucial that we establish the groundwork. Success in any side hustle starts with setting goals - clear, concise, and concrete objectives that will dictate your action plan. Without them, you're merely shooting in the dark, hoping your bullets land somewhere. To systematically build your wealth, first, you need to set your goals.

4.1. Identifying Your Financial Goals

The question that usually comes up when setting goals is, 'Where do I start?' Begin by acknowledging the current state of your finances. Examine your income, your savings, and your ability to invest in different opportunities. This self-assessment will give you an idea of the direction you want your side hustle to take.

Take some time to reflect and identify what you want to achieve financially. Are you looking to save for a house, pay off debts, or fund your child's education? Or do you want to supplement your income, start investing, or cultivate an emergency fund? Maybe you are eyeing that long overdue vacation, or you're dreaming of financial independence.

Once you know what you want to accomplish, write it down. Having your goals on paper makes them tangible and can help keep you accountable.

4.2. SMART Goals

Building on your list of financial objectives, you need to create SMART goals: Specific, Measurable, Achievable, Relevant, and Time-Bound.

Specific: Pinpoint what you wish to achieve. Vague goals often lead to vague results. For example, rather than stating you want to 'earn more money' from your side hustle, a specific goal would be 'I want to earn an additional $500 per month.'

Measurable: Develop a yardstick to measure your success. If your goal is to pay off debt, how much debt and by when?

Achievable: Make sure that your goal is realistic, within your capabilities, and achievable within your available resources. As much as you may aim for the stars, your goals should also reflect your current circumstances.

Relevant: Your goal should align with your long-term visions and values. For example, if your ultimate goal is to achieve financial freedom, your side hustle should be a vehicle that drives you towards that.

Time-Bound: Each goal must have a timeline. Deadlines act as a motivation and create a sense of urgency.

4.3. Strategic Planning

After setting your goals, you need to craft a plan of action - a strategy. This plan should guide your every move as you start and grow your side hustle.

Start by conducting market research on your chosen hustle. Understand the industry, your competitors, and your potential customers. Analyse the risks and determine how you will mitigate them. Think about your unique selling proposition (USP), the one thing that will set your business apart from others.

Next, create a budget. Working out how much money you need to start and maintain your side hustle will help keep you focused and financially responsible. Walk through any obstacles you might face and think about how you can overcome them.

Also, consider the time you can devote to your side hustle. It's crucial to factor in time for rest and recreation to avoid burnout.

4.4. Building Accountability

Accountability is key in achieving your goals. Share your goals with someone you trust and enlist their help in keeping you on track. Joining entrepreneurship clubs or accountability groups can also help. Staying accountable helps reinforce your commitments and keeps you from straying off the path.

Monitoring and evaluating your progress periodically is also essential. This reflection enables you to correct your course, make adjustments, and perpetually strive for progress.

4.5. Final Reflections

Remember, setting goals and following through with the required action is integral to any wealth-building strategy. These goals will form the foundation of your side hustle, providing the strategic direction you need to build a successful enterprise.

As you embark on this journey, remember that success does not happen overnight. It requires patience, perseverance, and consistent effort. Keep tweaking your goals, sharpening your skills, and pivoting as required. Before long, you'll see your side hustle flourish, proving that all the effort you've invested is worth its weight in gold.

There is no better time to set your goals and start paving your way to financial freedom than now. Keep your eyes on the prize, stick to your game plan, and success will follow. Don't let fear or uncertainty hold you back. Start today, and remember, the journey of a thousand miles begins with a single step. You're one decision away from a totally different life.

Chapter 5. Utilizing Skills and Interests: Finding Your Side Hustle Niche

Understanding one's unique blend of skills and interests is not just essential for career success; for the savvy entrepreneur, they can also be the perfect foundation for a lucrative side hustle. The process of identifying a side hustle niche is truly an exercise in self-discovery, where passions intersect with market needs to create a potential goldmine.

5.1. Know Thyself

Before venturing onto the path of side hustling, one should ask: "Who am I as a worker? As an individual? As a dreamer?" The key to finding your niche lies in knowing your skillset and interests. Some people possess an innate ability for creative pursuits like writing or design, while others shine in problem-solving, coding, or data analysis. Reflect on your professional and personal experiences and list the skills you have acquired and enjoyed using.

Next, consider your interests. Do you have hobbies or passions you can't get enough of? Perhaps you love fashion, gaming, or gardening. Maybe you're drawn to digital marketing, quantum computing, or financial planning. Identify the areas that captivate you. Undoubtedly, your passion will power your drive and commitment to make your side hustle successful.

5.2. Matchmaking: Skills, Interests, and Market Needs

After scrutinizing your skills and interests, you must map them onto market needs. Start by identifying market segments that align well with your special abilities and passions. For example, if writing is your strong suit and you're passionate about tech, you could consider a side hustle as a tech blogger or freelance writer for tech publications.

The key lies in understanding the market. Is there a need for your services? Who are your potential customers? What do they value? Are there existing competitors? How can you differentiate yourself? Our preliminary research should provide answers and guide you in establishing a unique value proposition for your side hustle.

5.3. Construct Your Value Proposition

The most successful side hustles are those that unequivocally provide value to their target audience. Use your understanding of the market to mold your skills and interests into a compelling value proposition.

For instance, suppose you're a spreadsheet whiz with an avid interest in personal finance. Your unique selling proposition could be creating customized budget and investment tracking templates for individuals wanting to take concrete steps towards financial independence. Your value proposition doesn't need to be earth-shattering; it simply needs to come from your strengths and address a need in the market.

5.4. Validating Your Niche

Every wise entrepreneur knows that assumptions should always be tested. Once you have identified your side hustle niche and crafted your unique value proposition, validate it.

Reach out to potential customers and colleagues for their feedback. Conduct surveys to understand your target audience's pain points and how your proposed solution may aid them. Getting constructive feedback early on will help save potentially wasted effort and resources. Remember, an idea validated by potential customers holds immense worth.

5.5. Build a Minimum Viable Product (MVP)

Now, set your wheels in motion. Create an MVP – a basic version of your product or service – and introduce it to a small segment of your target audience. This can be as simple as publishing a blog post, offering a seminar, launching a beta version of your app, or selling your handmade crafts at a local fair.

The feedback you gather from this can help refine your side hustle and position it for success. Building an MVP allows you to evaluate product-market fit, measure customer response, and make necessary adjustments before investing further.

5.6. Learning and Evolving

Remember that finding and establishing your side hustle niche is a process, one characterized by learning and evolving. You will encounter roadblocks, make mistakes, and undergo periods of uncertainty. But with perseverance and resilience, you will also experience growth, satisfaction, and success.

As you navigate your side hustle journey, continually reevaluate your situation. Are you still aligned with your skills and interests? Is the market responding positively? How can you pivot to better serve your audience and enrich your offerings? Be willing to adapt and evolve.

A fulfilling and profitable side hustle is more than just an additional source of income; it's a manifestation of your abilities, passions, and motivations. By leveraging your unique combination of skills and interests, you can create a side hustle that not only enriches your life financially, but also contributes positively to your personal growth, providing immense satisfaction and fulfillment along the way.

In the dynamic ecosystem of side hustles, the only constant is you – your skills, interests, and resolve to succeed. Your side hustle niche is waiting to be discovered, built, and nurtured. So, go ahead and seize the opportunity to create, innovate, and realize your entrepreneurial dreams!

Chapter 6. Balancing Act: Juggling Your Day Job and Side Hustle

For many, the idea of starting a side hustle while working a full-time job sounds overwhelming, even impractical. It's a concern that's best addressed with a careful dose of reality check and strategic know-how. After all, if almost half of all Americans can manage a side gig in addition to their full-time position, there's no reason you cannot do the same.

6.1. Understanding Your Time and Energy

First off, let's acknowledge the fact that working a full-time job and running a side business can be challenging. It requires a significant investment of your time, effort, and energy - resources that are already stretched thin due to your full-time commitments. This is where understanding your energy peaks and dips become crucial.

Recognize your peak productive hours. Are you more productive and energetic in the morning, afternoon, or at night? Align your side hustle tasks that call for the most brainpower and creativity accordingly. Optimizing your side hustle schedule according to your energy levels can dramatically improve your efficiency.

6.2. Setting Clear Boundaries

Drawing clear boundaries between your day job and your side venture ensures that neither occupation suffers due to the other. Hold your day job with the same seriousness post side hustle launch as before. It demands respect and commitment; after all, it's possibly the main source of your livelihood and might be funding your side hustle too.

Set boundaries in terms of time as well. Reserve specific blocks of time for your side hustle tasks. Avoid allowing your side business to spill over into your day job hours, not just out of professionalism but also to promote a healthier work-life balance.

6.3. Prioritizing and Delegating

To effectively manage your full-time job and side hustle, you must learn to prioritize your tasks and delegate when possible. List out all tasks, categorize them based on urgency and importance, and address them accordingly.

One smart move would be to invest in tools that can automate certain tasks. Automation can take the burden off repetitive, mundane tasks, freeing up your time for strategic decision-making and creativity.

When your side hustle starts generating a decent income, consider outsourcing certain tasks too. The idea is to focus on what you do best and delegate the rest.

6.4. Embracing the Power of 'No'

The more things you commit to, the less time you will have for your side hustle. Learn to say 'No' to things that do not align with your life goals or do not contribute significantly to your happiness or well-being. Remember, every 'Yes' is a 'No' to something else. Make sure you are prioritizing wisely.

6.5. Building a Support Network

Another crucial part of juggling a full-time job and side hustle is building a support network. This can include family, friends, mentors, or like-minded entrepreneurs who understand your journey and can provide emotional, mental, and even financial support. Joining communities of other side hustlers can also help you learn from others' experiences, get advice, share knowledge, and stay motivated.

6.6. Maintaining Your Health and Wellness

Above all, don't forget to take care of your physical and mental well-being. Eat healthily, exercise regularly, get enough sleep, and take breaks when necessary. It's easy to get caught up in the hustle and forget about the most essential factor that determines your success – your health.

In conclusion, balancing a full-time job and a side hustle is genuinely a challenging act. However, with meticulous planning, strategic delegation, judicious time management, proper prioritization, and a strong support system, it can indeed become a rewarding experience leading to financial independence and fulfilling professional growth.

Chapter 7. Money Matters: Funding Your Side Hustle

Let's begin unravelling the intricacies of funding your side hustle. Initiating a side hustle requires upfront investment. Whether small or large, you need capital for many purposes, starting from purchasing inventory to marketing. The right mix of funds can be your rocket-fuel to launch and sustain your entrepreneurial journey.

7.1. What Do You Really Need?

Assess what you genuinely require to start your project. More often than not, aspiring entrepreneurs tend to overestimate or underestimate their business needs, leading to financial and operational hurdles in the long run. Take a holistic approach and calculate the comprehensive amount needed. This includes operational costs, marketing expenditure, inventory procurement, contingencies, and more.

7.2. Understand Your Funding Options

Once you have a rough estimate, look at the financial resources available to you. There are several innovative ways to finance your side hustle. While personal savings seem to be the easiest route, don't bypass the potential of bootstrapping, crowdfunding, angel investors, small business loans, and so forth.

7.3. Bootstrapping

Bootstrapping, or self-funding, is typically the first step a side hustler can take. Harness your existing capital, be it your savings, salary, or investments, to fund your project. However, bear in mind, the risks involved as you're spending your safety net.

7.4. Crowdfunding

Crowdfunding is another excellent option for side hustlers. Platforms like Kickstarter or GoFundMe provide crowdfunding opportunities. Here, you pitch your idea to the audience who, if interested, would fund your project in exchange for product samples, swag, etc.

7.5. Angel Investors

While angel investors typically focus on high-growth startups, some choose to invest in ambitious side hustles. Here, experienced entrepreneurs offer a lump sum in exchange for a percentage equity in your business. This arrangement not just brings investment but valuable industry experience from your investor.

7.6. Small Business Loans

Small business loans might be difficult to procure initially, but with a sound business plan and promising trajectory, lenders may be willing to bet on your side project.

7.7. Pursuing Financial Stability

Achieving financial stability is a continuous process that goes hand in hand with scaling your business or side hustle. Strategies, such as regularly reviewing your financial status, saving for taxes, adopting excellent bookkeeping habits, and hiring financial assistance (accountants or financial advisors) when required, could be game-changer.

7.8. Investment in Inventory and Equipment

Procuring inventory and necessary equipment effectively is also a crucial aspect of financial management for your side hustle. Explore different vendors, do your research, and negotiate to get the best rates possible.

7.9. Marketing and Promotion

A side hustle could be the next big thing, but it's hard to let the world know about it without marketing. Investment in marketing and promotions can significantly impact your reach and customer acquisition.

7.10. The Contingency Plan

Let's face it, entrepreneurship is not without its snags and hitches. Unplanned circumstances or crises may arise. Having a contingency fund will ensure you're equipped to handle unexpected expenditures, keeping your side hustle running smoothly.

7.11. Expanding Your Side Hustle

When your side hustle starts to show profitability, it might be time to take it to the next level. Expansion requires additional funding and an altered financial strategy. Be prepared to invest more, but also be ready to reap more rewards.

7.12. Conclusion

Funding your side hustle might seem like a challenging endeavor, but with careful planning and a healthy understanding of money matters, you can navigate your way towards financial stability. Remember, a well-funded side hustle isn't the sole factor for success. It's about combining it with dedication and a savvy business strategy for optimum results.

Invest consciously, spend wisely, and make your side hustle a prosperous venture. This chapter benefits aspiring side hustlers with a crunchy grasp on the monetary aspects associated with starting and nurturing a side business. So, keep going, fund your side hustle wisely, and take one more step towards your financial independence today.

Chapter 8. Marketing Your Ambition: Brand Building Strategies

Understanding the significance of your brand in your side hustle is essential for marketing your ambition efficiently. Far from being a superficial aesthetic choice, your brand is the foundation of your business identity. It communicates your business values, personality, and what sets you apart from your competition. This chapter will delve deeper into brand-building strategies that will help propel your side hustle into a sustainable revenue stream.

8.1. The Core Philosophy of your Brand

Getting clear on the underlying philosophy of your brand is an initial and essential step in the process. It's not just about products or services you are offering but the values and mission that drive your brand. Ask yourself, why do you do what you do? What difference do you want to make? What is the narrative surrounding your venture?

Think about your motivation behind starting your side hustle. Your motivation is a compelling aspect that can create a unique brand identity. Be authentic and transparent in your communication. Customers tend to relate more to brands that they find honest and transparent.

8.2. Identifying your Target Audience

Understanding who your target audience is, is a crucial factor in building your brand. You need to know who you're talking to in order to tailor your messaging and branding strategy effectively. Understand the demographics and psychographics of your audience. Demographics refer to age, location, gender, occupation, etc., while psychographics refer to their interests, values, behaviors, and attitudes.

For instance, if you're offering tutoring services, your target audience could be parents of school-going children, and your marketing message should appeal to their concern for their child's academics. In contrast, if you are developing a mobile app for fitness enthusiasts, you need to understand their workout habits, motivations, pain points, and workout goals.

8.3. Designing your Brand Aesthetics

Once you are clear on your brand's core philosophy and have identified your target audience, the next step is to design your brand aesthetics. This includes your logo, color scheme, typography, the look and feel of your website, product packaging, and any other visual elements. Consistency in visuals helps derive a strong brand recall. Make sure that your aesthetics are aligned with your target audience's preferences.

For example, if your side hustle is about sustainable products, you might choose earthy tones for your color scheme to reflect the natural environment.

8.4. Creating a Unique Value Proposition (UVP)

A UVP is basically your promise—the unique identifier that sets you apart from your competition. It articulates the unique benefits that customers can expect from your product or service, why they should choose you over your competitors, and backs up these claims with proof.

Your UVP should be clear, concise, customer-focused, and demonstrate your knowledge about your market and competition. It is an excellent tool to attract your audience and persuade them to invest in your offerings.

8.5. Crafting a Compelling Brand Story

Branding isn't just about aesthetics or catchy slogans; it's also about your story. Stories help build an emotional connection with your audience. A compelling brand story communicates your journey, struggles, successes, and vision in an engaging manner. Be real, be relatable, and touch your audience's emotions with your story. This emotional connection can do wonders in fostering brand loyalty and driving sales.

Remember, your story isn't what you tell people it is, it's what people tell each other it is.

8.6. Utilizing Social Media for Branding

Social media is an excellent tool to reach out to your target audience and create a strong brand presence. Each platform has its own demographics and style, so figure out where your audience hangs out online and focus on those platforms.

Regularly post engaging content that adds value to your audience. Contests, Q&A sessions, stories, infographics, behind-the-scenes shots, customer testimonials, and educational posts are some of the ways to engage your audience on social media. Use hashtags relevant to your side hustle to expand your reach.

8.7. Building Brand Partnerships

On your journey to building a powerful brand, don't hesitate to collaborate with other brands that share a similar audience. Brand partnerships can help you reach a wider audience and also add value to your existing audience by offering them something unique.

Partnership could be in the form of guest blog posts, social media shoutouts, hosting events together, or offering combined services or products.

8.8. Consistency is Key

The golden rule of branding is consistency. Whether it's your messaging, your aesthetics, your story, or your social media posts—being consistent is the key. Consistency helps in cultivating a strong brand identity that customers can remember and relate to. An inconsistent brand can be confusing for the customers and dilutes brand impact.

Branding is an ongoing process and needs updating with developments in your offerings, changes in your target audience's preferences, or evolving market trends. However, the core should remain consistent while the layer on top could be adaptive and dynamic.

Building a strong brand takes time, but with patience and consistent efforts, you can successfully turn your side hustle into a brand that resonates with your audience and helps secure your financial independence.

Chapter 9. Scaling Up: Taking Your Side Hustle To New Heights

A side hustle is more than just a way to make some extra cash; it's an opportunity to build a business and secure future prosperity. Taking your side hustle to the next level requires careful planning, diligent effort, and a variety of practical strategies. So, how do you make that transition from a side gig to a thriving empire? This comprehensive guide will provide you with the wealth-building strategies required to elevate your side hustle.

9.1. Identifying Your Growth Potential

Before scaling up, you must understand your current state and the potential for growth in your business. This requires a hard look at your operations, customer base, financials, and products or services. Determine what your unique value proposition is and how it resonates with your target audience. Once you've identified the growth potential, you can craft a strategic plan for scaling your side hustle.

9.2. Developing Your Strategic Plan

Your strategic plan should outline your vision, mission, and goals. It should also include specific, measurable, achievable, relevant, and time-bound (SMART) objectives to guide your business growth. Your plan should define your success metrics, timelines, as well as identify potential obstacles and the strategies you'll use to overcome them.

. Strategic Plan Format Example

Vision: Your long-term perspective for your business

Mission: What your business aims to achieve now

Goals: Broad outcomes you aim to realize

Objectives: Measurable steps to reach your goal

Strategies: Actionable steps to achieve your objectives

9.3. Crafting a Strong Value Proposition

Your value proposition is a unique combination of products or services that sets you apart from competitors. To scale your hustle, you need a compelling value proposition that appeals to a broad customer base. Listen to your customers and learn from their feedback to refine your offering.

9.4. Upgrading Your Skills and Capabilities

Scaling a side hustle demands more from your repertoire of skills and capabilities. Whether it's marketing, sales, finance, or operations: you might need to upgrade your skills or bring in additional talent to handle these areas. Consider online courses, workshops or hiring freelancers to fill out the skill gaps in your enterprise.

9.5. Building Systems and Processes

Efficiency is crucial as you scale, and this is where systems and processes become essential. The repetition of tasks within business operations becomes common as you grow, and having established processes can reduce time, increase efficiency, and promote a consistent output quality.

9.6. Embracing Technology

Technology can streamline your operations, making your business more efficient and scalable. Identify the areas of your business that may benefit from technological integration. Whether it's a customer relationship management system, digital marketing tools or e-commerce platforms, technology can provide leverage in managing and growing your business.

9.7. Building A Strong Brand

As your business grows, you need to invest in building a robust brand. This not only includes a memorable logo and website but also encapsulates the total customer experience. Your brand should reflect your mission and values and resonate with your target audience.

9.8. Developing a Comprehensive Marketing Strategy

Marketing is not just about promotion but also entails understanding your customer's needs, their behaviors, and the market trends. It involves positioning your product or service in a way that appeals to your target audience. Social media marketing, email campaigns, content marketing, and search engine optimization (SEO) are some of the effective digital marketing strategies to embrace.

9.9. Financing Your Growth

Taking your side hustle to the next level may necessitate additional financial resources. Different financing methods exist, such as bootstrapping, crowdfunding, venture capital, or bank loans. Evaluate the approach that best suits your business's needs and growth phase.

9.10. Seeking Professional Advice

Professionals like accountants, lawyers, and business consultants can provide advice and insights that aid your business's growth. Consider seeking their expertise to navigate through legal, tax, and business challenges you may encounter as you scale up your side hustle.

Scaling your side hustle takes time, dedication, and the right strategies. By following the guidance provided in this exhaustive guide, you can position your business for success. Remember, the journey to building a successful business is not always a straight line; it has ups and downs. Patience, persistence, and a growth mindset are crucial traits to foster as you embark on this exciting journey.

Chapter 10. Minimizing Risks and Overcoming Challenges

Turning a side hustle into a successful wealth-building strategy does not come without its own set of potential stumbling blocks. Acknowledging these challenges and learning how to effectively navigate them is crucial for an entrepreneur. In this chapter, we will delve into practical techniques for minimizing risks and overcoming challenges, offering a roadmap for managing the ups and downs of your wealth-building journey.

10.1. Assessing Risks in Your Side Hustle

An essential first step is identifying potential risks associated with your side hustle. Whether you're selling a physical product, offering a service, or generating revenue through affiliate marketing, it's important to understand what could potentially go wrong. This can include factors such as market demand, cost increases, supply chain disruptions, and more. By identifying these risks early on, you can devise strategies to address them, should they come to fruition.

An effective approach to assess risks is to perform a SWOT analysis. SWOT stands for Strengths, Weaknesses, Opportunities, and Threats. This analysis will help you understand your business assets, the potential gaps, opportunities to tap into, and potential threats to be aware of.

```
| Strengths | Weaknesses |
| Opportunities | Threats |
```

10.2. Developing a Risk Management Plan

Once you have identified potential risks, the next step is to develop a risk management plan. This plan should address each identified risk and provide a course of action that you can take to mitigate the damaging effects of those challenges.

Your risk management strategy can include things like diversifying your income streams, creating emergency savings, or getting business insurance. You might also consider implementing contingencies in your supply chain if you're producing a physical product.

For example, if you're starting an online tutoring side hustle, a potential risk could be a decrease in demand during the summer months. To mitigate this risk, you might diversify your income by also offering consulting services or courses.

```
| Identified Risk | Mitigation Strategy |
| Decrease in demand during summer | Diversify income
with consulting services |
```

10.3. Overcoming Challenges and Obstacles

Likewise, becoming a successful entrepreneur requires a unique ability to overcome the numerous challenges and obstacles you may face.

The first step to overcoming challenges is to stay flexible and adaptable. The business environment is constantly changing, and your ability to adapt and evolve with it places you in the best position to successfully navigate obstacles.

Persistence is another key attribute. It is easy to get discouraged by setbacks, but remember that all entrepreneurs face hurdles. The difference between those who ultimately succeed and those who fail is often the ability to persist through the challenges and maintain a positive, problem-solving mindset.

10.4. Learning From Mistakes

No entrepreneurial journey is complete without making a few mistakes. Rather than viewing these as failures, regard them as an opportunity to learn and grow. Digest the lessons they offer and apply this knowledge as you move forward. Always remember, the most successful entrepreneurs are those who have learned from their missteps.

10.5. Building a Support Network

A strong support network is an invaluable asset. Surrounding yourself with like-minded individuals can provide not only moral support but can also provide helpful advice, different perspectives, and valuable contacts.

Cultivating a strong network, attending entrepreneur-focused events and workshops, and joining online communities can all contribute to your ability to successfully navigate the world of side hustles.

10.6. Embracing Change and Innovation

Lastly, it's crucial to remain open to change and innovation. This mindset will enable you to keep up with market trends and needs, and continue to adapt your side hustle accordingly. Stay alert to emerging technologies and evolving customer behaviours, and seek to employ these trends to offer a product or service that continually satisfies and exceeds market needs.

Remember, the path to entrepreneurial success isn't always smooth, but with thorough risk assessment, effective risk management, an adaptable attitude, a thirst for learning, and robust support, you're well-equipped to handle the challenges that come your way. Embrace the obstacle-filled journey, for the rewards are undoubtedly worth it.

Chapter 11. Securing Your Future: Wealth Management and Growth

Having a side hustle is just the beginning. The end game is to grow your wealth and secure your future. This effort calls for strategic and thoughtful planning. With this in mind, in this chapter we take you through comprehensive wealth management and growth strategies to aid your journey towards financial independence.

11.1. Understanding Wealth Management

Wealth management is not just about earning money. It involves strategically growing, protecting, and utilizing your assets. Planning is crucial because it helps you outline your financial goals and direct your efforts towards achieving them.

To start understanding wealth management, you must know your current financial position. Complete a comprehensive evaluation of your assets. This includes your income, savings, investments, property, and any other items of value. Be thorough and include everything. With this knowledge, you can start creating a roadmap for wealth growth.

11.2. The Power of Compound Interest

Albert Einstein once called compound interest "the eighth wonder of the world." But why is it so powerful? Simply put, compound interest means earning interest on your interest. The principle can fairly accelerate your wealth growth if you intelligently utilize it. By continuously reinvesting your earnings, you benefit from a virtuous cycle of increasing returns.

11.3. Diversify Your Portfolio

"Diversification" is a buzzword in the investment world that isn't taken seriously enough. By spreading investments across various assets (stocks, bonds, real estate, and others), you reduce the risk associated with putting "all your eggs in one basket." More significant diversification indicates less exposure to a single asset's performance and hence less risk. It immensely strengthens your portfolio.

11.4. Budgeting: A Key to Wealth Management

Budgeting gives you control over your financial state, allowing you to make informed decisions. Create a budget that reflects your income, living costs, savings, and investments. Set clear limits for discretionary expenses, so you don't run into unnecessary debts. Remember, a budget is only as effective as your commitment to sticking to it.

11.5. Debt Management

Wealth cannot be discussed without addressing debt. In essence, minimizing your debt is part of managing your wealth. Be strategic in dealing with your debts. Prioritize high-interest debts and work consistently towards paying them off.

11.6. Automating Your Finances

In this digital era, you can let technology do the heavy lifting.

Automating your savings helps eliminate the potential human error of missing a month's contribution or a temptation of spending instead of saving.

11.7. Investing In Your Education

Another significant way to secure your future is investing in your knowledge and skills. The more skilled and knowledgeable you are, the more income streams you can generate, hence diversifying your portfolio further.

11.8. Creating an Emergency Fund

Unexpected expenses can have a significant impact on your financial status. Having an emergency fund provides a safety net, protecting against those unforeseen expenses without disrupting your wealth growth plan.

11.9. Protection through Insurance

Insurance plays a critical role in wealth management. It provides a protective shield against potential financial setbacks brought about by unexpected life events.

11.10. Building for Retirement

Your retirement should be as sustainable as your working years. This is where planning becomes critical. A robust retirement plan is a robust wealth growth plan. Understanding and enrolling into the suitable retirement plans could save you a lot of financial distress in later years.

11.11. Estate Planning

Wealth management doesn't cease when you're gone. It's about ensuring your wealth is distributed among those you leave behind in accordance with your wishes. This requires drafting a comprehensive will and designating trusted executors.

Wealth management might seem complicated in the beginning. However, with consistent effort, it gets clearer, and navigating your financial future becomes less daunting. Solid financial planning is an investment in your future. Therefore, take the time to understand it, and you'll be well on your way to creating stable, long-term wealth. Remember that the first step is always the hardest, but with the right mindset and guidance, you'll be ready to walk on the path of financial independence. You have the power to turn your financial dreams into reality. Believe in yourself and make that first move toward securing your future.

www.ingramcontent.com/pod-product-compliance
Lightning Source LLC
Chambersburg PA
CBHW071034260726
48661CB00007B/3022